Best Friends Forever

Keepsake Journal With Prompts for Best Friends

Dedication

This Best Friends Journal is dedicated to all the best friends out there who want to share thoughts, memories, goals with their best friend and document their findings in the process.

You are my inspiration for producing books and I'm honored to be a part of keeping all of your Best Friends notes and records organized.

This journal notebook will help you record your details about your friendship.

Thoughtfully put together with these sections to record in detail: What Makes A Best Friend, Write An Adventure Story The Two Of You Go On, Draw Your Best Friends Face, Write A Poem About Your Best Friend, and much more!

How to Use this Book

The purpose of this book is to keep all of your Best Friend notes all in one place. It will help keep you organized.

This Best Friends Journal will allow you to accurately document every detail about your friendship. It's a great way to chart your course through a long lasting friendship.

Here are examples of the prompts for you to fill in and write about your experience in this book:

1. Blank lined space for you to write what makes a best friend

2. Write an adventure story the two of you go on together

3. Draw your best friends face

4. Write a poem about your best friend

5. Make a playlist you want to play for their birthday party

6. List your favorite movies you've watched together

7. A bucket list for the two of you

8. Your favorite memories together

What makes a "Best Friend"?

Write a story about you and your best friend going on an adventure.

Write a story about you and your best friend going on an adventure.

Stare at your best friend for 4 minutes (don't forget to time it!). Draw sketches of each other's faces. Capture whatever strikes as the most unique or interesting features of your friend's face.

Stare at your best friend for 4 minutes (don't forget to time it!). Draw sketches of each other's faces. Capture whatever strikes as the most unique or interesting features of your friend's face.

List 10 favorite things about each other
(personality, traits, physical quirks, or just
anything that makes your best friend special)

1. _____

2. _____

3. _____

4. _____

5. _____

6. _____

7. _____

8. _____

9. _____

10. _____

List 10 favorite things about each other
(personality, traits, physical quirks, or just
anything that makes your best friend special)

1. _____

2. _____

3. _____

4. _____

5. _____

6. _____

7. _____

8. _____

9. _____

10. _____

Write a poem about your best friend's qualities

Write a poem about your best friend's qualities

What do you do when you disagree with your best friend?

What do you do when you disagree with your best friend?

Create a playlist for your best friend's awesome birthday bash. What songs MUST be played? Don't forget to include your favorites too!

List your all-time favorite movies EVER that you watched and enjoyed together.

_____

_____

_____

_____

_____

_____

_____

_____

_____

_____

Write a story about 2 friends who are separated when one moves away. How do they continue their friendship?

Write a story about 2 friends who are separated when one moves away. How do they continue their friendship?

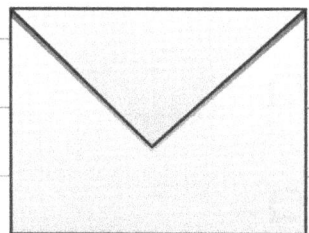

_____

_____

_____

_____

_____

_____

_____

_____

_____

_____

_____

_____

_____

_____

_____

_____

A bucket list of things I want to do with my best friend

❏ _____

❏ _____

❏ _____

❏ _____

❏ _____

❏ _____

❏ _____

❏ _____

❏ _____

❏ _____

❏ _____

❏ _____

A bucket list of things I want to do with my best friend

❑ _____

❑ _____

❑ _____

❑ _____

❑ _____

❑ _____

❑ _____

❑ _____

❑ _____

❑ _____

❑ _____

List your favorite places that you like going to with your best friend. What do you do there?

_____

_____

_____

_____

_____

_____

_____

_____

_____

_____

_____

_____

_____

_____

_____

_____

_____

_____

List your favorite places that you like going to with your best friend. What do you do there?

Write down the cutest things you've ever seen your crush wear.

Write down the cutest things you've ever seen your crush wear.

On this page and the next, you and your best friend fill in the blanks. Compare answers afterwards.

My favorite **holiday** is _____

because I'm totally **obsessed** with

_____

and really **can't stand**

_____.

My current **Bestest Friend** is _____

He / She is **special** to me because

_____.

When I think about _____, I feel

butterflies in my stomach because _____

_____

_____.

On this page and the next, you and your best friend fill in the blanks. Compare answers afterwards.

My favorite **holiday** is _____

because I'm totally **obsessed** with

_____

and really **can't stand**

_____.

My current **Bestest Friend** is _____

He / She is **special** to me because

_____.

When I think about _____, I feel

butterflies in my stomach because _____

_____

_____.

Pics of my best friend and I

Pics of my best friend and I

Write your favorite memories with your best friend.

Write your favorite memories with your best friend.

TRIVIA

Write things that only YOU know about your best friend

_____

_____

_____

_____

_____

_____

_____

_____

_____

_____

_____

_____

_____

_____

TRIVIA

Write things that only YOU know about your best friend

_____

_____

_____

_____

_____

_____

_____

_____

_____

_____

_____

_____

_____

_____

_____

_____

QUIZ!!! Answer the following and let your best friend check if it's correct or wrong.

	Correct	Wrong
Favorite color:		
Favorite food:		
Favorite subject:		
Favorite outfit:		
Favorite sports:		
Favorite song:		
Favorite music genre:		
Favorite movie:		
Annoyances:		
Good mood triggers:		
Foot size:		
Future aspiration:		
Motivators:		
First crush:		

QUIZ!!! Answer the following and let your best friend check if it's correct or wrong.

	Correct	Wrong
Favorite color:		
Favorite food:		
Favorite subject:		
Favorite outfit:		
Favorite sports:		
Favorite song:		
Favorite music genre:		
Favorite movie:		
Annoyances:		
Good mood triggers:		
Foot size:		
Future aspiration:		
Motivators:		
First crush:		

What's the worst thing that's happened to you and how did your best friend help you out?

What's the worst thing that's happened to you and how did your best friend help you out?

What was your first impression of your best friend?

What was your first impression of your best friend?

List 10 of your favorite school lunch items

1.

2.

3.

4.

5.

6.

7.

8.

9.

10.

List 10 of your favorite school lunch items

1.

2.

3.

4.

5.

6.

7.

8.

9.

10.

List 10 of your LEAST favorite school lunch items

1.

2.

3.

4.

5.

6.

7.

8.

9.

10.

List 10 of your LEAST favorite school lunch items

1.

2.

3.

4.

5.

6.

7.

8.

9.

10.

What do you do when someone is being mean to your best friend?

What do you do when someone is being mean to your best friend?

What would make your best friend feel loved by you?

_____

_____

_____

_____

_____

_____

_____

_____

_____

_____

_____

_____

What would make your best friend feel loved by you?

What does it mean to be a "true friend"?

What does it mean to be a "true friend"?

What's the nicest thing that your best friend has done for you?

_____

_____

_____

_____

_____

_____

_____

_____

_____

_____

_____

_____

_____

_____

What's the nicest thing that your best friend has done for you?

Draw a caricature of your best friend.

Draw a caricature of your best friend.

What are some things you've learned from your best friend?

What are some things you've learned from your best friend?

How can you show appreciation for your friend on a daily basis?

_____

_____

_____

_____

_____

_____

_____

_____

_____

_____

_____

How can you show appreciation for your friend on a daily basis?

Why are friends so valuable?

Why are friends so valuable?

Draw an award for your best friend.

Draw an award for your best friend.

If I could give my best friend a Christmas gift, it would be a... because....

_____

_____

_____

_____

_____

_____

_____

_____

_____

_____

_____

_____

If I could give my best friend a Christmas gift, it would be a... because....

If I could give my best friend a birthday gift, it would be a... because....

_____

_____

_____

_____

_____

_____

_____

_____

_____

_____

If I could give my best friend a birthday gift, it would be a... because....

_____

_____

_____

_____

_____

_____

_____

_____

_____

_____

Qualities that you admire about your best friend

Qualities that you admire about your best friend

How can I be a better friend?

How can I be a better friend?

Write a story about going on a trip with your friend.

Write a story about going on a trip with your friend.

Have you and your best friend gotten into trouble together? What did you do?

Have you and your best friend gotten into trouble together? What did you do?

Can friends ever be like family? Why?

_____

_____

_____

_____

_____

_____

_____

_____

_____

Can friends ever be like family? Why?

Write a letter to your best friend.

Write a letter to your best friend.

What makes your friendship unique from others?

What makes your friendship unique from others?

Summer activities you like doing together

Autumn activities you like doing together

Winter activities you like doing together

Spring activities you like doing together

What's the perfect halloween costume for your best friend? Draw it.

What's the perfect halloween costume for your best friend? Draw it.

Collage more pics with your best friend. Decorate each page.

Collage more pics with your best friend. Decorate each page.

Collage more pics with your best friend. Decorate each page.

Collage more pics with your best friend. Decorate each page.

What's your wish for your best friend?

What's your wish for your best friend?

What are the responsibilities of friendship?

What are the responsibilities of friendship?

How do you solve misunderstandings with your best friend?

_____

_____

_____

_____

_____

_____

_____

_____

_____

_____

_____

_____

_____

How do you solve misunderstandings with your best friend?

_____

_____

_____

_____

_____

_____

_____

_____

_____

_____

_____

_____

Draw a symbol of your friendship.

Draw a symbol of your friendship.

Explain why you drew that symbol.

_____

_____

_____

_____

_____

_____

_____

_____

_____

_____

_____

_____

Explain why you drew that symbol.

_____

_____

_____

_____

_____

_____

_____

_____

_____

_____

_____

How do you see your friendship 10 years from now?

How do you see your friendship 10 years from now?

This journal has been completed by:

_____

and

_____

www.ingramcontent.com/pod-product-compliance
Lightning Source LLC
Chambersburg PA
CBHW051032030426
42336CB00015B/2835